The Lady J Stress-Reset Worksheet

Created by
Lady J Holistic Wellness

Disclaimer

This worksheet is intended for personal reflection and educational purposes only. It is not a substitute for professional medical or mental health advice.

"This material may not be reproduced, distributed, or resold without written permission."

You can contact the author

For seminars, Workshops, and trainings at the following:

shela.charlot@ladyjholisticwellness.com

www.ladyjholisticwellness.com

Dedication

This work is born from love, loss, resilience, and becoming.

To my beloved husband, Jean-Yves (Jay)

thank you for being my greatest supporter, my safe place, and my constant source of encouragement. You believed in me in ways I didn't always believe in myself. Your love continues to guide me, and this work is a reflection of everything we built together. I carry you with me in every step of this journey.

To my children, Jon and JJ

you are my reason, my motivation, and my pride. Watching you grow, persevere, and honor your father's legacy fills my heart in ways words cannot fully express.

To my granddaughter

thank you for bringing light, love, and laughter into my life, especially during a year that tested me deeply. You are a reminder that joy still exists, even in the midst of grief.

A special and heartfelt thank you to my sisters at heart, Suzeline Michel and Nirva Louis

your unwavering love, support, and presence over the past five years have carried me through some of

the most challenging moments of my life. I am forever grateful for you both.

This journey has not been easy, but it has been meaningful.

And through it all, I have learned that even in the deepest pain, there is space to heal, to grow, and to begin again.

With love,

Lady J 

About the Author

Shela D. Charlot, known as Lady J, is a Licensed Certified Social Worker, Certified Life Coach, and Wellness & Transformation Consultant dedicated to helping women reset, heal, and realign their lives with intention.

With a professional background rooted in human services, education, and clinical social work, Shela brings a unique blend of therapeutic insight, practical tools, and compassionate guidance to every space she creates. She has spent years supporting individuals and families through life's most complex challenges, meeting people where they are and guiding them toward sustainable growth, clarity, and emotional wellbeing.

Shela is also the visionary behind Lady J Wellness & Life Transformation; a brand created from both professional experience and personal evolution. Following the loss of her husband, Jean-Yves (Jay), she transformed her grief into purpose, building a platform that honors healing, resilience, and the power of beginning again. Through her work, she creates safe, structured, and empowering environments where women can release emotional weight, rebuild confidence, and step into the next chapter of their lives.

Her offerings include the Lady J Reset, a 12-week transformational coaching experience, corporate wellness workshops focused on burnout and sustainability for helping professionals, and curated wellness events designed to foster connection, reflection, and renewal.

At her core, Shela believes that healing does not require perfection, only permission. Permission to pause, to feel, to grow, and to become.

When she is not working, Shela enjoys reading, spending time outdoors, and creating meaningful moments with her family. She is a proud mother and grandmother, and she carries her life experiences into her work with authenticity, grace, and strength.

✦ Reset. Rise. Restore. ✦

Welcome to your Lady J Wellness Journey.

This worksheet was created to give you a daily space to reconnect with yourself. Life moves quickly, and many women spend their days caring for others while neglecting their own needs.

This worksheet is your daily invitation to pause, breathe, reflect, and reset.

Through intentional journaling, affirmations, and mindfulness practices, you will begin to:

- Strengthen emotional awareness

- Reduce stress and overwhelm

- Reconnect with your purpose

- Cultivate self-worth and confidence

- Create a life aligned with your wellness goals

Just a few minutes each day can create a powerful transformation.

With love,

Lady J

Worksheet 1

The Stress Trigger Identifier

What situation triggered my stress?

What thoughts came up?

What emotions did I feel?

- ☐ Anger
- ☐ Anxiety
- ☐ Sadness
- ☐ Fear
- ☐ Frustration

Describe what it feels like.

Gratitude

Gratitude

Worksheet 2

Body Awareness Scan

Where do I feel stress in my body?

- ☐   Head
- ☐   Neck
- ☐   Shoulders
- ☐   Chest
- ☐   Stomach
- ☐   Back

Describe what it feels like.

Gratitude

Gratitude

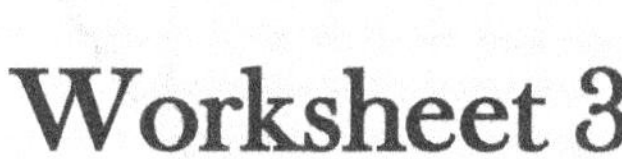

Worksheet 3

The Reset Plan

When stress appears, I will:

- ☐   Pause and breathe
- ☐   Step away from the situation
- ☐   Talk to someone supportive
- ☐   Journal my thoughts
- ☐   Take a short walk
- ☐   Practice grounding

My personal reset strategy:

Gratitude

Gratitude

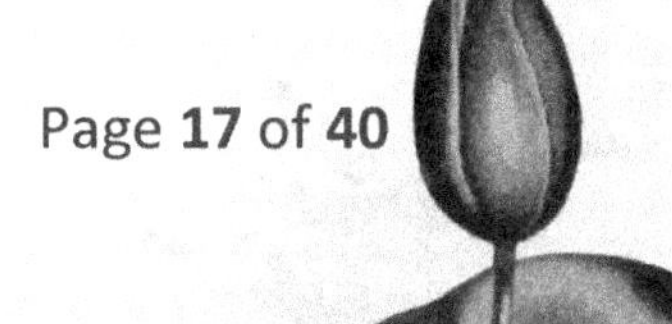

Worksheet 4

Reframing Negative Thoughts

Negative Thought:

Is this thought 100% true?

- ☐ Yes

- ☐ No

If healthier thought could be:

Gratitude

Gratitude

Worksheet 5

Emotional Release Exercise

What emotion do I need to release?

What would help release it?

- ☐ Cry
- ☐ Journal
- ☐ Talk it out
- ☐ Exercise
- ☐ Rest

Gratitude

Gratitude

Worksheet 1

The Stress Trigger Identifier

What situation triggered my stress?

What thoughts came up?

What emotions did I feel?

- ☐ Anger

- ☐ Anxiety

- ☐ Sadness

- ☐ Fear

- ☐ Frustration

Describe what it feels like.

Gratitude

Gratitude

Worksheet 2

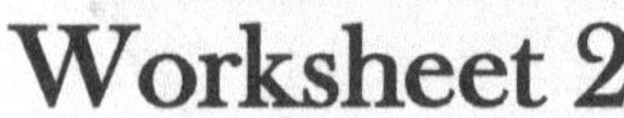

Body Awareness Scan

Where do I feel stress in my body?

- ☐   Head
- ☐   Neck
- ☐   Shoulders
- ☐   Chest
- ☐   Stomach
- ☐   Back

Describe what it feels like.

Gratitude

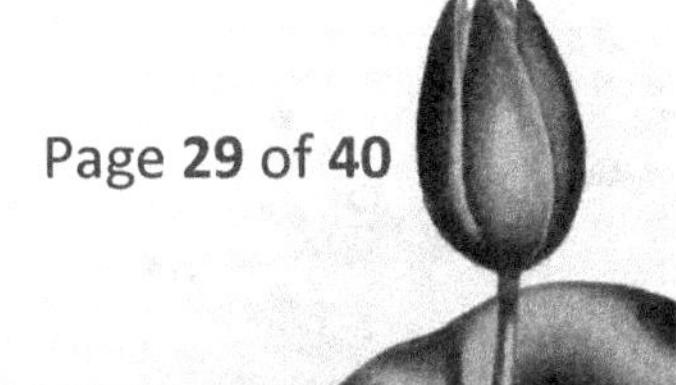

Gratitude

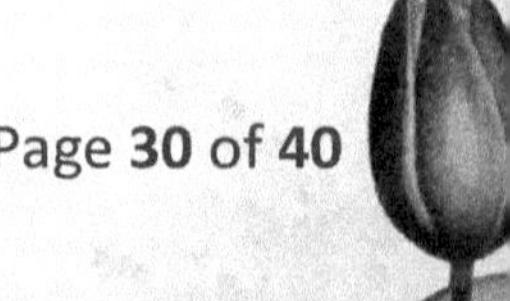

Worksheet 3

The Reset Plan

When stress appears, I will:

- ☐ Pause and breathe

- ☐ Step away from the situation

- ☐ Talk to someone supportive

- ☐ Journal my thoughts

- ☐ Take a short walk

- ☐ Practice grounding

My personal reset strategy:

Gratitude

Gratitude

Worksheet 4

Reframing Negative Thoughts

Negative Thought:

Is this thought 100% true?

- ☐ Yes

- ☐ No

If healthier thought could be:

Gratitude

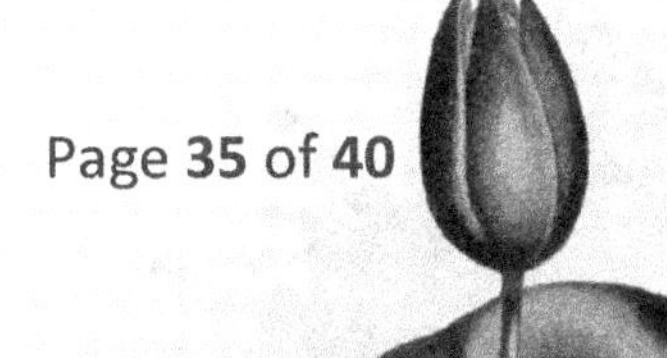

Gratitude

Worksheet 5

Emotional Release Exercise

What emotion do I need to release?

What would help release it?

- ☐ Cry
- ☐ Journal
- ☐ Talk it out
- ☐ Exercise
- ☐ Rest

Gratitude

Gratitude